OSCAR BERG

THE DEAD HORSE THEORY

ILLUSTRATED

CREATED BY OSCAR BERG
oscarberg.net

STICK FIGURES BY LEREMY GAN
leremy.com

PUBLISHER: Gr8 Mountains AB, Lund, Sweden
PRINT: BoD – Books on Demand, Norderstedt, Germany
ISBN: 978-91-988415-4-1

The tribal wisdom of the Dakota Ppople, which has been passed on from generation to generation, states that "when you discover that you are riding a dead horse, the best strategy is to dismount."

According to the Dead Horse Theory, in modern business, education, and government, it is common to use advanced strategies in an attempt to revive dead horses.

This book illustrates over 60 strategies, as well as tips on how to identify a dead horse.

DISCLAIMER: No horse was harmed in the creation of this book. Animals are not ours to harm or abuse simply because we can.

"In order to succeed, we must first recognize that we have failed"

— Unknown

#1 FIND MOTIVATION

BUY A STRONGER WHIP

#2 INCREASE THE MOTIVATION

THREATEN THE HORSE WITH TERMINATION

#3 CHANGE RIDERS

A NEW RIDER CAN BRING FRESH PERSPECTIVES AND IDEAS

#4 FORM A COMMITTEE

APPOINT A COMMITTEE TO STUDY THE HORSE

#5 LOOK FOR BEST PRACTICES

ARRANGE TO VISIT OTHER COUNTRIES TO SEE HOW OTHERS RIDE DEAD HORSES

#6 UPDATE STANDARDS

**LOWER THE STANDARDS SO THAT DEAD HORSES
CAN BE INCLUDED**

#7 RECLASSIFY

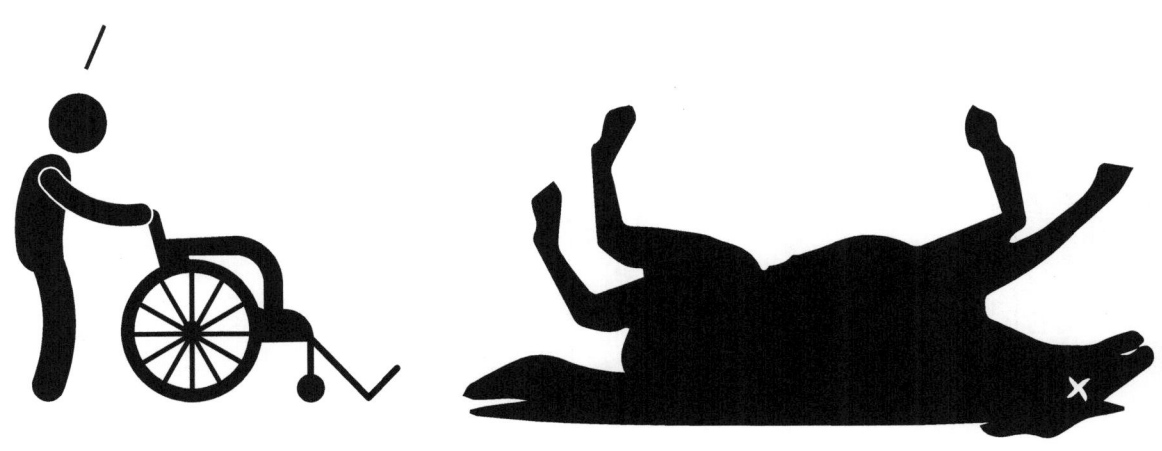

RECLASSIFY THE DEAD HORSE AS 'LIVING-IMPAIRED'

#8 HIRE OUTSIDE CONTRACTORS

HIRE OUTSIDE CONTRACTORS TO RIDE THE DEAD HORSE

#9 CREATE SYNERGIES

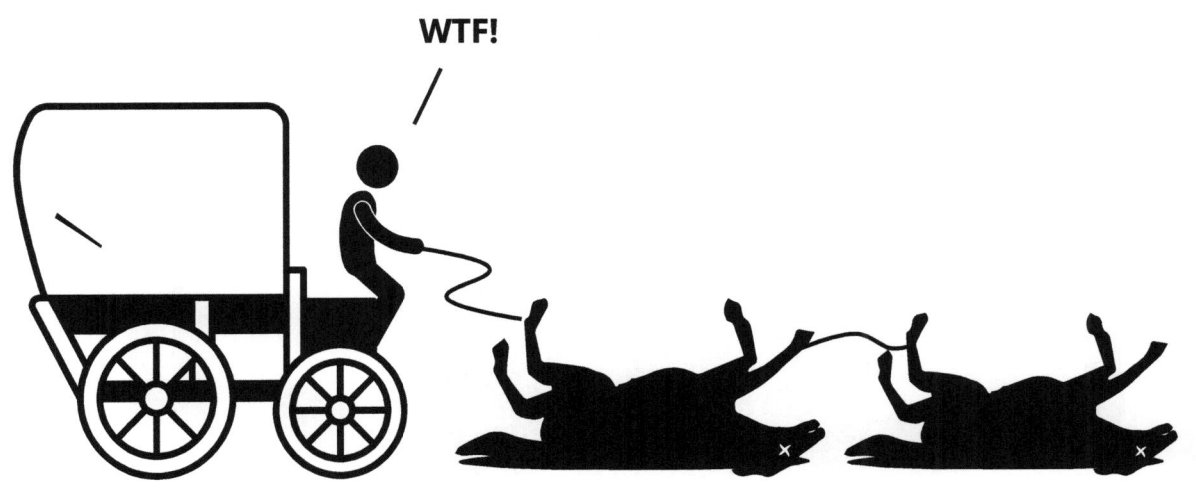

HARNESS SEVERAL DEAD HORSES TOGETHER TO
INCREASE THE SPEED

#10 INVEST MORE

PROVIDING ADDITIONAL FUNDING AND/OR TRAINING TO INCREASE THE DEAD HORSE'S PERFORMANCE

#11 STUDY PRODUCTIVITY

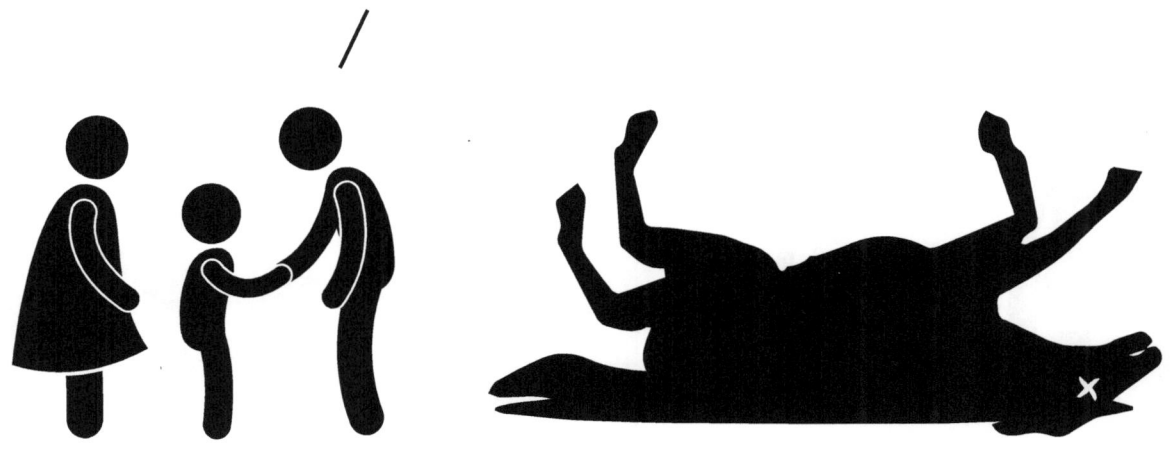

CONDUCT A PRODUCTIVITY STUDY TO SEE IF LIGHTER RIDERS WOULD IMPROVE THE DEAD HORSE'S PERFORMANCE

#12 FOCUS ON THE BENEFITS

THE DEAD HORSE DOESN'T HAVE TO BE FED, IT'S LESS COSTLY, CARRIES LOWER OVERHEAD AND, THEREFORE, CONTRIBUTES SUBSTANTIALLY TO THE BOTTOM LINE

#13 UPDATE THE KPIS

RE-WRITE THE EXPECTED PERFORMANCE REQUIREMENTS FOR ALL HORSES

#14 ANNOUNCE A PROMOTION

PROMOTE THE DEAD HORSE TO A SUPERVISORY POSITION OF HIRING ANOTHER HORSE

#15 PRACTICE STRATEGIC IGNORANCE

LET YOUR MIND PUSH AWAY INFORMATION THAT GETS IN THE WAY OF YOUR DESIRE FOR THE HORSE TO BE ALIVE

#16 MODERNISE

DO MODERN THINGS, SUCH AS HIRING INFLUENCERS TO MAKE
THE DEAD HORSE LOOK COOL AND TRENDY AGAIN

#17 OUTSOURCE

OUTSOURCE THE DEAD HORSE TO A COUNTRY WHERE MANUAL LABOUR CAN REPLACE HORSEPOWER

#18 USE CREATIVE ACCOUNTING

FIND LOOPHOLES IN ACCOUNTING STANDARDS TO HIDE THE NEGATIVE CONSEQUENCES OF THE DEAD HORSE

#19 USE AS TARGET OF BLAME

USE THE DEAD HORSE AS A SCAPEGOAT FOR EVERYTHING
THAT'S GOING WRONG WITH THE BUSINESS

DEAD
Since
1999
Aged to
PERFECTION
LIMITED EDITION

PROCLAIM THAT THE BUSINESS IS BASED ON A LONG AND A PROUD TRADITION OF RIDING DEAD HORSES

#21 DIGITIZE

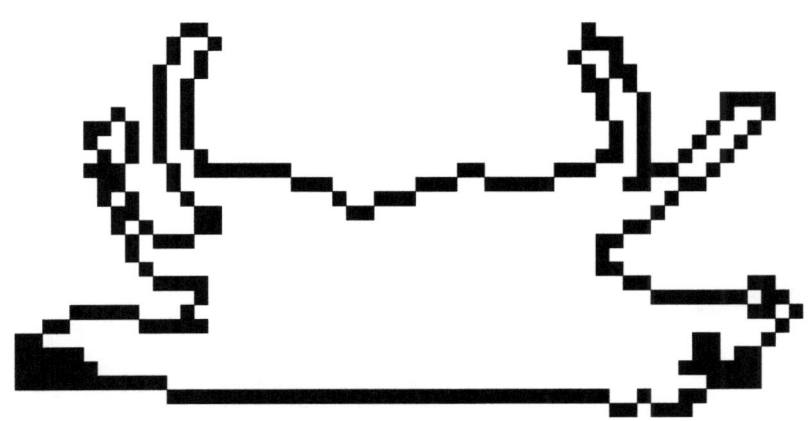

**DIGITIZE THE HORSE SO IT CAN BE PROGRAMMED
BACK TO LIFE**

#22 BLAME THE PANDEMIC

**BLAME THE DEATH OF THE HORSE ON THE PANDEMIC — SEEK
FUNDING FROM A COVID-19 ECONOMIC RELIEF PROGRAM**

#23 APPOINT A CDHO

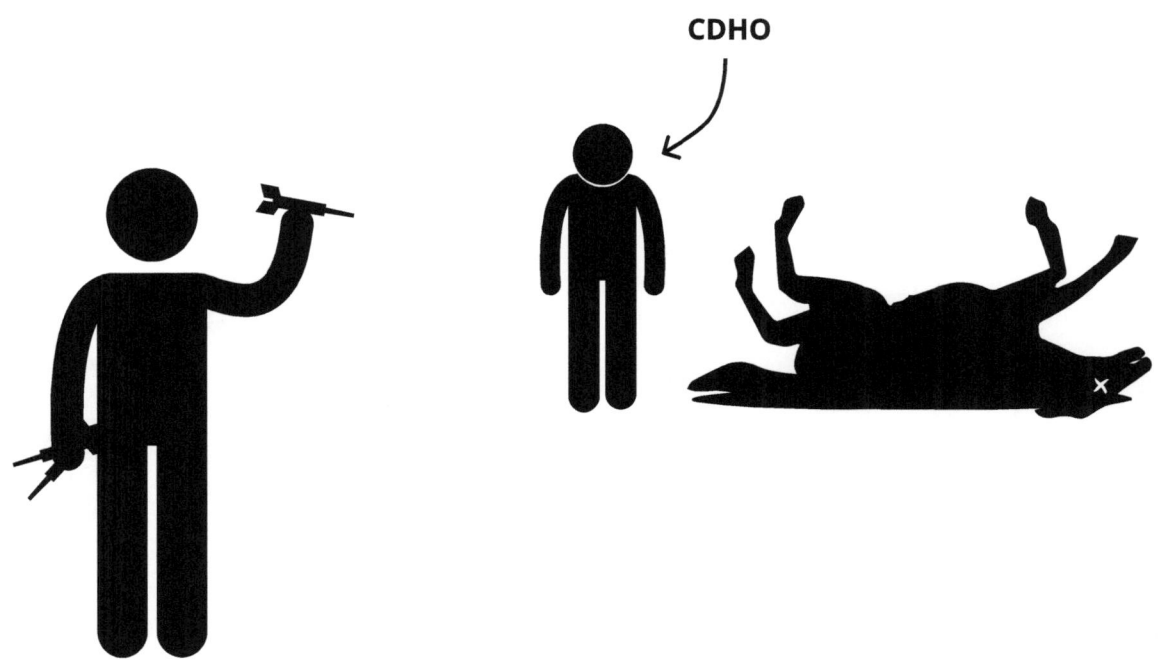

APPOINT A CHIEF DEAD HORSE OFFICER (CDHO), AND MAKE
HIM OR HER TAKE ALL THE BLAME FOR THE DEAD HORSE

#24 TRY AGAIN

MAKE A NEW HORSE THE SAME WAY AS YOU MADE THE DEAD ONE, HOPING FOR A DIFFERENT RESULT

#25 FIND WORKAROUNDS

CIRCUMVENT THE PROBLEMS CAUSED BY THE DEAD HORSE WITH VARIOUS 'TEMPORARY' FIXES

#26 LAUNCH A TRANSFORMATION PROGRAM

LAUNCH A MULTI-YEAR TRANSFORMATION PROGRAMME RUN BY A MAJOR CONSULTANCY

#27 ADOPT NEW TECH

INVEST IN EXPENSIVE NEW TECHNOLOGIES THAT CAN BRING
THE DEAD HORSE BACK TO LIFE, SUCH AS VIRTUAL REALITY

#28 INNOVATE

LAUNCH NEW AND SEEMINGLY INNOVATIVE INITIATIVES TO SHIFT EVERYONE'S FOCUS AWAY FROM THE DEAD HORSE

#29 RUN FOCUS GROUPS

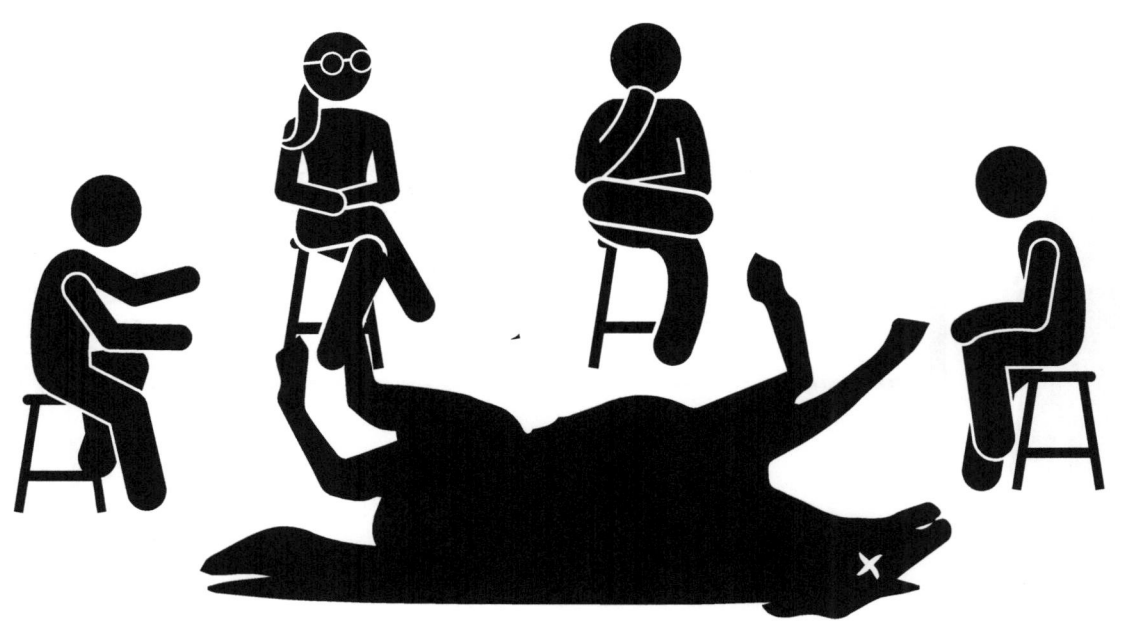

**RUN FOCUS GROUPS TO DISCUSS WHETHER
THE HORSE IS DEAD OR NOT**

#30 REORGANIZE

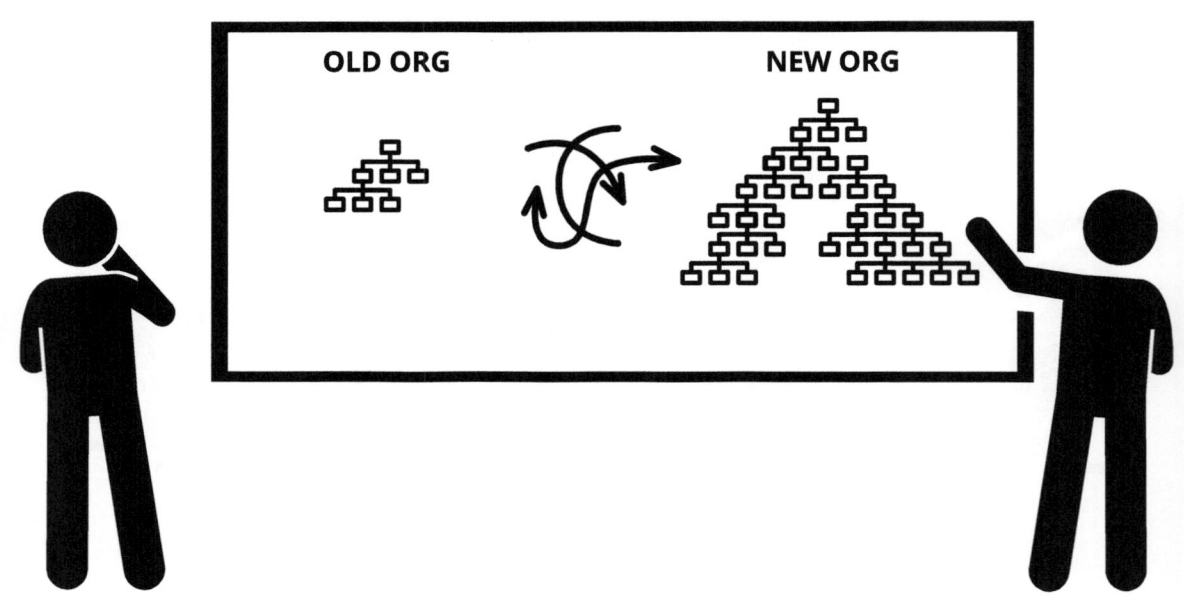

MAKE A COMPLETE OVERHAUL OF THE ORGANISATION'S INTERNAL STRUCTURE TO REVIVE THE DEAD HORSE

#31 BENCHMARK

COMPARE THE HORSE WITH OTHER DEAD HORSES AND CONCLUDE THAT IT PERFORMS NO WORSE THAN THEM

#32 REVERT TO OFFICE POLITICS

USE THE DEAD HORSE TO SPICE UP OFFICE POLITICS

#33 USE ARTIFICIAL INTELLIGENCE

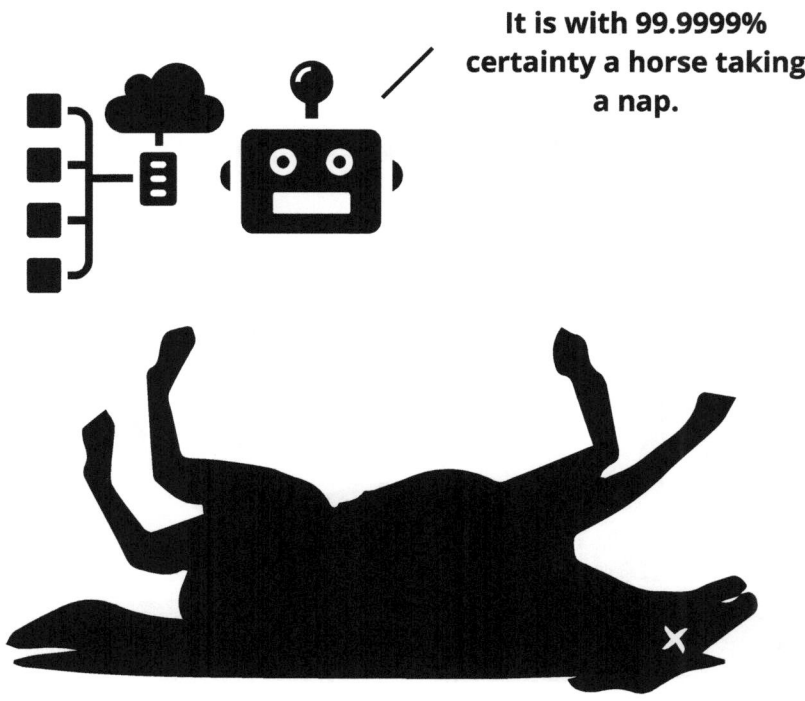

It is with 99.9999% certainty a horse taking a nap.

LET AN AI GO THROUGH 3.42 ZILLION DATA POINTS
COLLECTED THROUGHOUT THE HORSE'S LIFE

#34 FIND A NEW PURPOSE

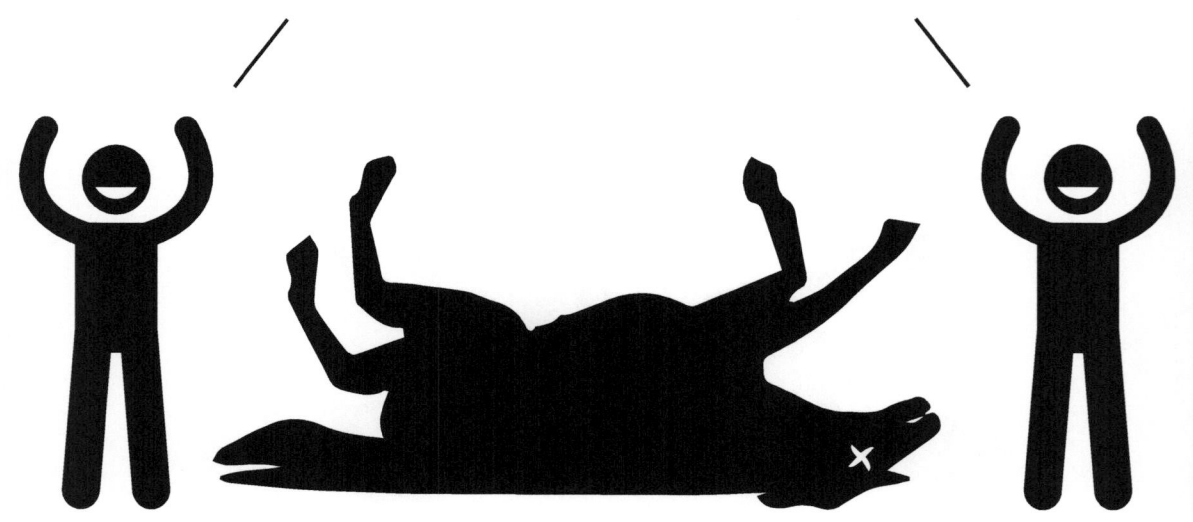

FIND A NEW PURPOSE AND TRY TO ACHIEVE IT BY SAYING IT OUT LOUD TO EVERYONE YOU MEET

#35 LABEL AS BETA VERSION

CLAIM THAT THE DEAD HORSE IS CURRENTLY IN THE BETA DEVELOPMENT STAGE, INDEFINITELY

#36 DO A REBRANDING

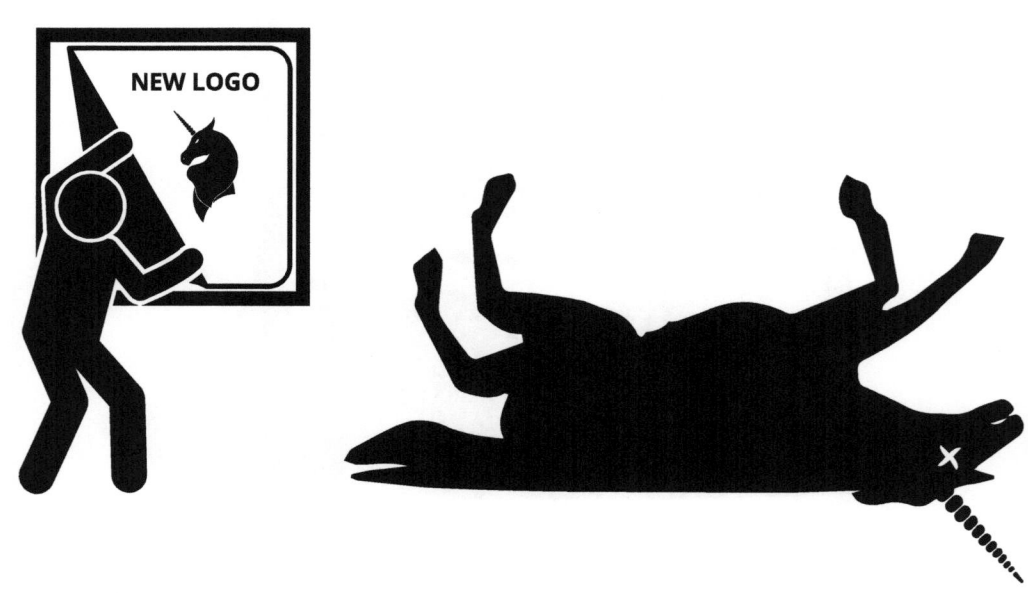

REBRAND THE DEAD HORSE AS A (DEAD) UNICORN

#37 CHANGE THE NARRATIVE

THE HORSE MAY BE DEAD, BUT IT OUTPERFORMS ALL LIVING HORSES IN TERMS OF CARBON EMISSIONS

#38 PROVIDE ADDED VALUE

LAUNCH VALUE-ADDED PRODUCTS AND SERVICES THAT WILL MAKE THE DEAD HORSE MORE ATTRACTIVE

#39 TRANSFER OWNERSHIP

TRANSFER THE OWNERSHIP (A.K.A. THE BLAME) OF THE DEAD HORSE TO ANOTHER DEPARTMENT

#40 REPLENISH THE TEAM

Fresh resources

Depleted resources

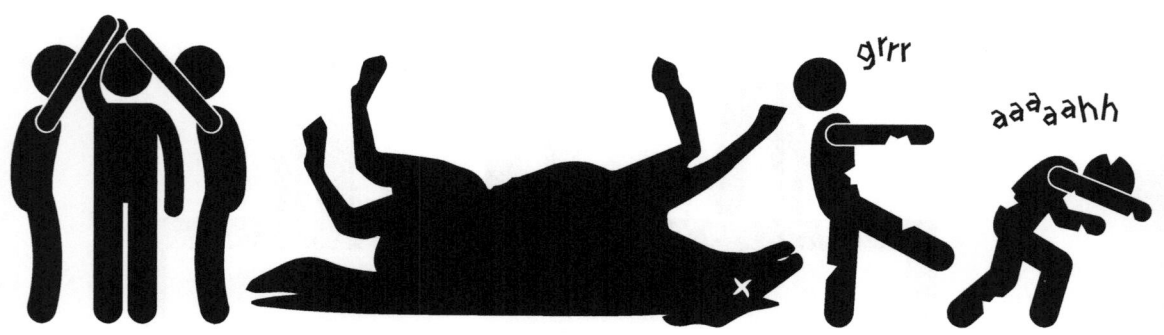

BRING IN FRESH NEW RESOURCES THAT CAN REVIVE THE DEAD HORSE

#41 RESET

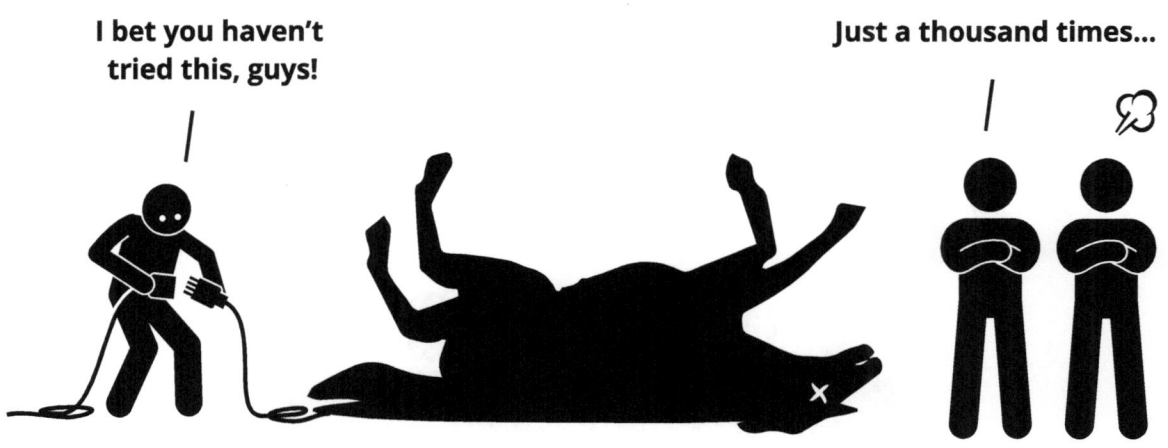

BRING SOMEONE IN FROM ANOTHER LOCATION TO CONNECT THE DEAD HORSE TO THE POWER SUPPLY

#42 PERFECT THE PITCH

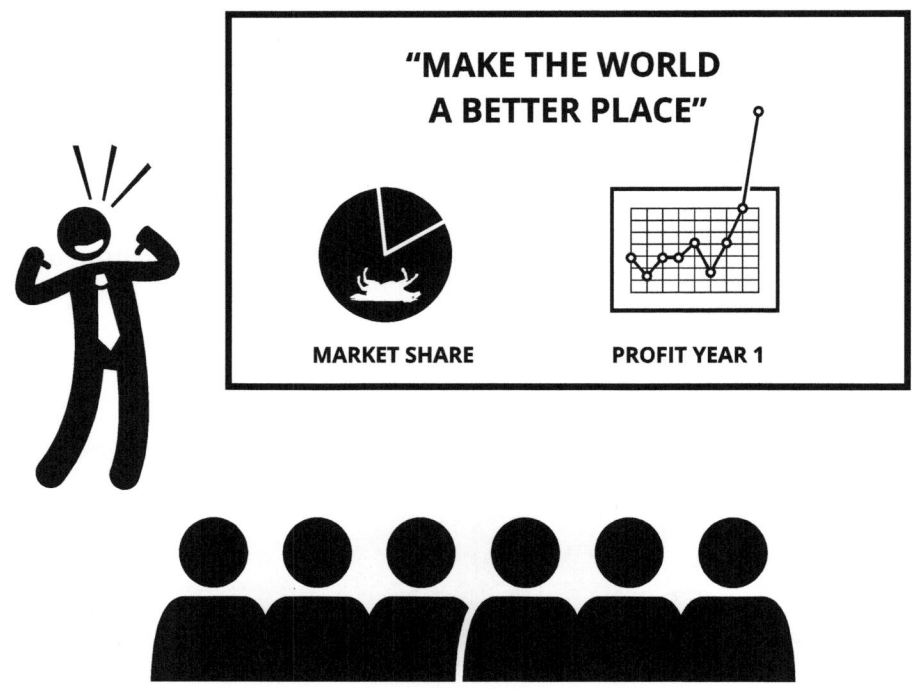

CONVINCE INVESTORS THAT DEAD HORSES ARE 'THE FUTURE OF THE BUSINESS'

#43 INJECT BUZZWORDS

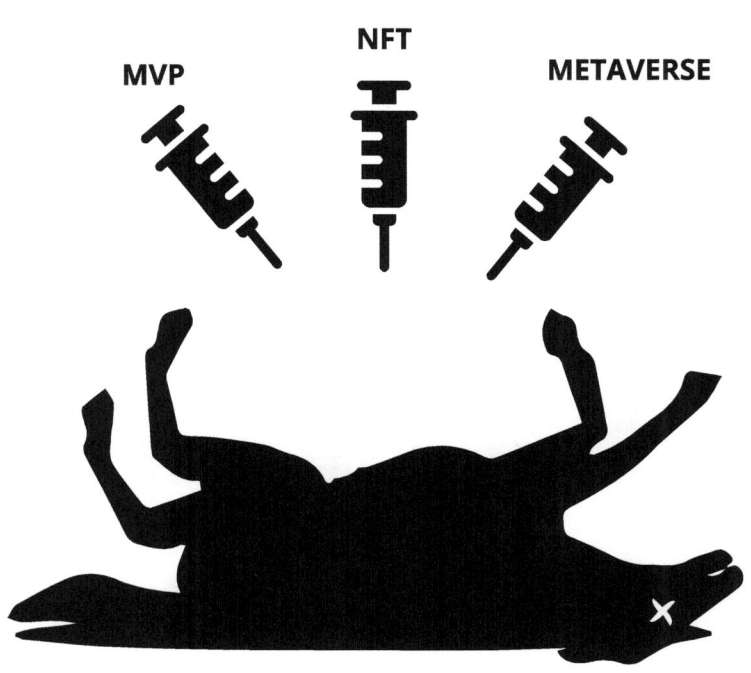

MEDICATE THE DEAD HORSE WITH
ALL SORTS OF COOL NEW TERMS

#44 PIVOT

**MAKE NFT:S AND CRYPTO ART OF THE DEAD HORSE
AND MAKE EXCLUSIVE DROPS**

#45 GO WITH THE FLOW

DO LIKE THE DEAD HORSE – RELAX AND GO WITH THE FLOW!

#46 IMPLEMENT NEW METHODOLOGY

CHOOSE ANY OFF-THE-SHELF METHODOLOGY SUCH AS LEAN, SIX SIGMA OR AGILE, AND APPLY IT TO THE DEAD HORSE

#47 CREATE A REALITY DISTORTION FIELD

REFUSE TO ACCEPT THE LIMITATIONS OF THE DEAD HORSE AND BELIEVE THAT ALL DIFFICULTIES CAN BE OVERCOME

#48 FAIL TO SUCCEED

KEEP RIDING THAT DEAD HORSE, BECAUSE FAILURE IS AN IMPORTANT STEP TOWARDS SUCCESS

#49 SCALE UP

**BRING AS MANY ADDITIONAL RESOURCES AS POSSIBLE
ON BOARD THE DEAD HORSE TO SAVE IT**

#50 GROW TOO BIG TO FAIL

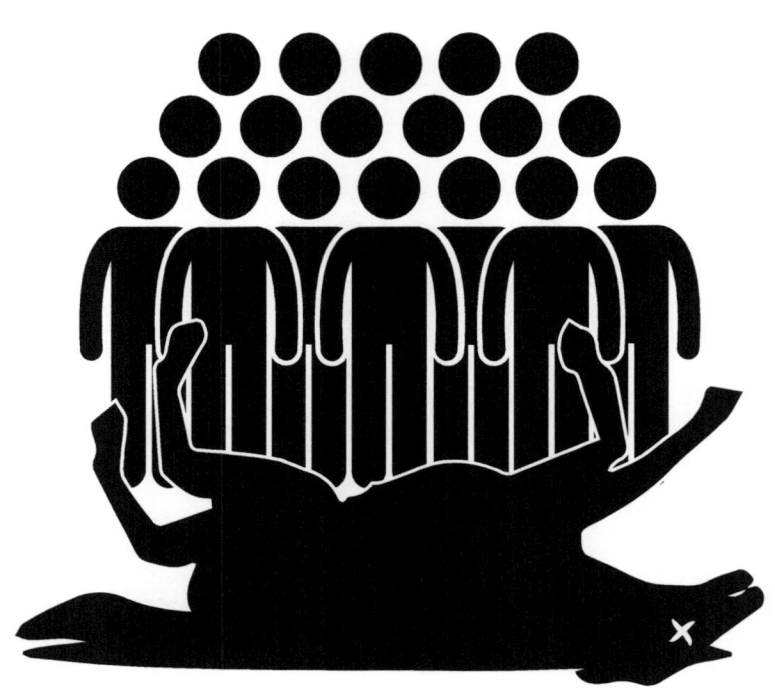

MAKE THE DEAD HORSE SO LARGE FAILING WOULD BE DISASTROUS TO THE GREATER ECONOMIC SYSTEM, AND THAT IT THEREFORE MUST BE SUPPORTED BY GOVERNMENTS

#51 CONDUCT RANDOM LAYOFFS

LAY OFF A RANDOM BUT SIGNIFICANT PERCENTAGE OF THE WORKFORCE TO PLEASE THE STOCK MARKET

#52 PUT IT IN A BOX

HIDE THE DEAD HORSE IN A SCHRÖDINGER'S BOX, SO THAT NOBODY KNOWS IF IT IS DEAD OR NOT

#53 ADD NEW INCENTIVES

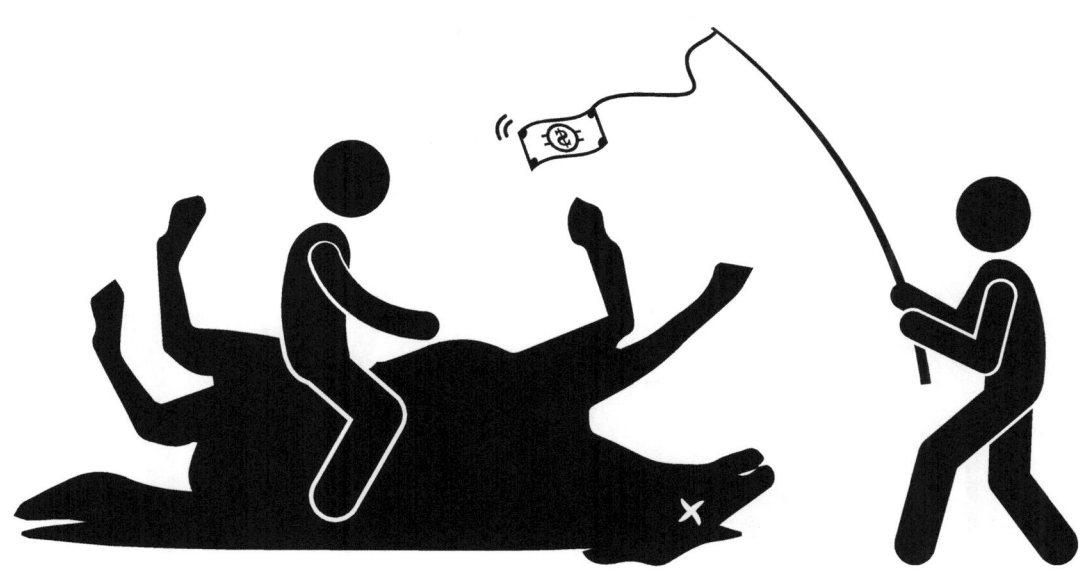

**PROVIDE MORE INCENTIVES TO MAKE THE RIDER
MORE MOTIVATED TO RIDE THE DEAD HORSE**

#54 FOCUS ON THE WHY

FOCUS ON THE WHY (WHY MOVE AT ALL?) INSTEAD OF FOCUSING ON THE WHAT (THE DEAD HORSE) AND THE HOW (HOW TO MAKE IT MOVE)

#55 DECLARE A NEW NORMAL

DECLARE THAT DEAD HORSES ARE THE NEW NORMAL

#56 CHANGE BUSINESS MODEL

INTRODUCE A SUBSCRIPTION MODEL INSTEAD OF REQUIRING CUSTOMERS TO BUY THE DEAD HORSE

#57 FOCUS

**THE CORE OF THE STRATEGY IS TO CHOOSE WHAT NOT TO DO
- GET RID OF EVERYTHING BUT THE DEAD HORSE**

#58 MOVE TO THE CLOUD

MOVE THE DEAD HORSE TO THE CLOUD TO TAKE ADVANTAGE OF THE CLOUD'S BENEFITS

#59 BEFRIEND STARTUPS

ESTABLISH 'STRATEGIC PARTNERSHIPS' WITH COOL STARTUPS TO MAKE THE DEAD HORSE FEEL LESS DEAD

#60 CREATE AN APP

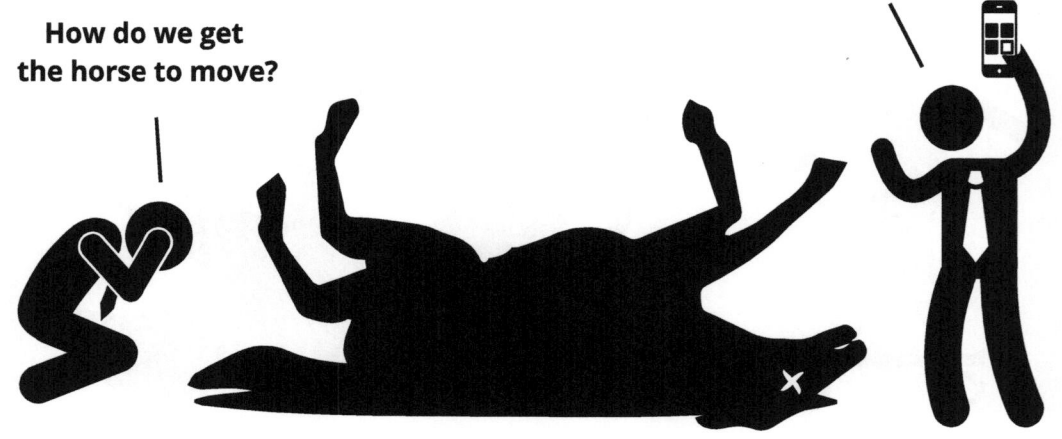

IF YOU JUST DEVELOP AN APP FOR THE DEAD HORSE, THE DEAD HORSE WILL NO LONGER BE A PROBLEM

#61 WORK HARDER

IF YOU JUST WORK HARDER, CHANCES ARE THE DEAD HORSE CAN COME BACK TO LIFE

"However beautiful the strategy, you should occasionally look at the results"

– Sir Winston Churchill

HOW TO SPOT
A DEAD HORSE?

#1 LACK OF PROGRESS

THE HORSE IS NOT PRODUCING THE DESIRED RESULTS

#2 DECREASED ENTHUSIASM

**TEAM MEMBERS ARE NO LONGER ENGAGED
OR PASSIONATE ABOUT THE HORSE**

#3 CONSISTENT FAILURE

THE HORSE CONSISTENTLY FAILS TO MEET ITS GOALS OR TARGETS

#4 STRESS OR BURNOUT

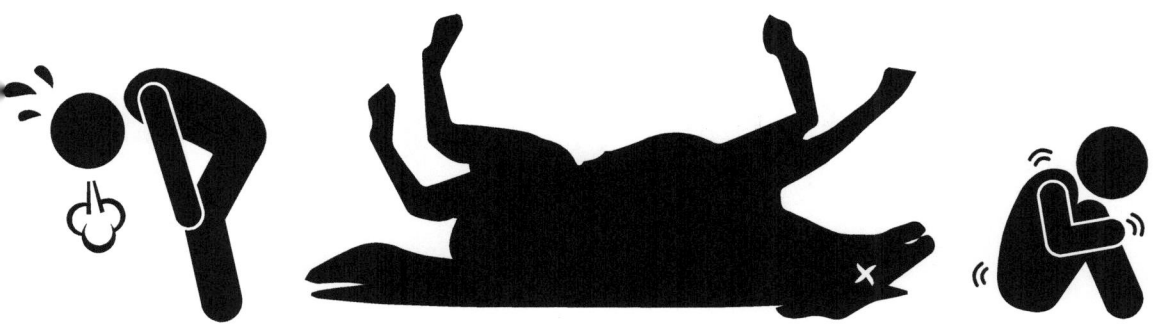

TEAM MEMBERS ARE EXPERIENCING HIGH LEVELS OF STRESS OR BURNOUT

#5 LACK OF INTEREST

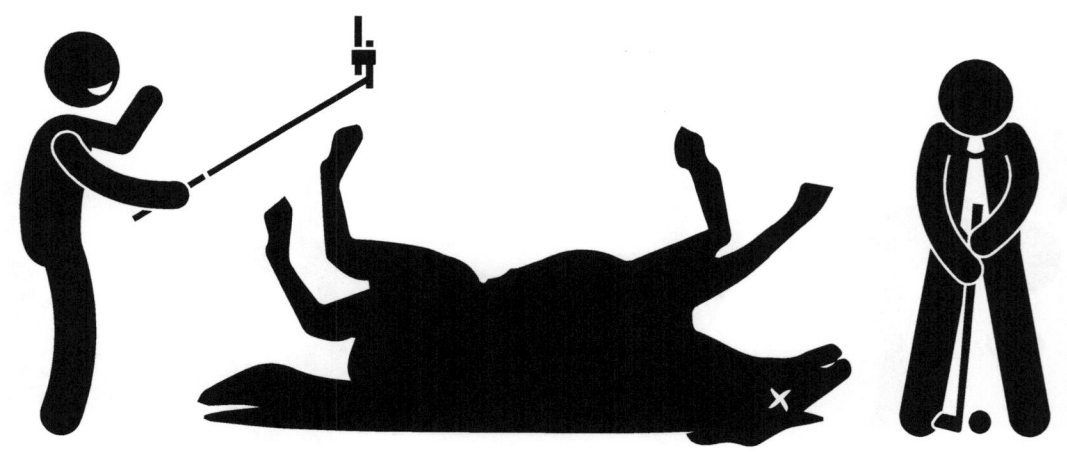

**STAKEHOLDERS OR TEAM MEMBERS HAVE
LOST INTEREST IN THE HORSE**

#6 NEGATIVE ROI

THE RETURN ON THE DEAD HORSE IS NEGATIVE

#7 CHANGES IN THE MARKET

SIGNIFICANT CHANGES IN THE MARKET MAKE CONSUMERS INTERESTED IN OTHER THINGS THAN DEAD HORSES

#8 MISSED DEADLINES

DEADLINES ARE CONSISTENTLY MISSED

"We can't solve problems by using the same kind of thinking we used when we created them."

— Albert Einstein

IS OFFICE WORK
A DEAD HORSE?

When considering data on productivity for remote versus office work, it's possible that the office is becoming obsolete. According to research by Global Workplace Analytics, remote American Express workers produced 43% more than their office-based counterparts.[1] Furthermore, workplace distractions can cause businesses to lose up to USD 600 billion annually.[2]

If the office is becoming obsolete, then the notion that knowledge work must be carried out at an office is a dead horse. Despite this, many employers use a variety of strategies, ranging from basic to sophisticated, to encourage employees to return to the office. Here are a few examples of such strategies.

#1 USE AUTHORITY

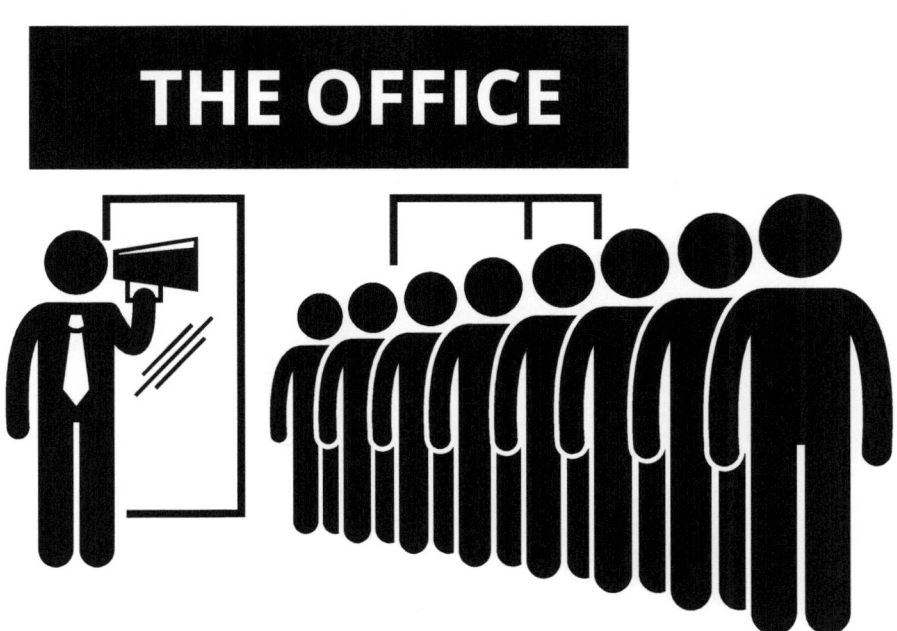

COMMAND ALL EMPLOYEES BACK TO THE OFFICE

#2 INCREASE IT SECURITY

PREVENT EMPLOYEES FROM ACCESSING IT SYSTEMS OUTSIDE THE OFFICE FOR 'SECURITY REASONS'

#3 MAKE WFH A BENEFIT

**PRESENT THE OPPORTUNITY TO WORK FROM HOME
AS AN EMPLOYMENT BENEFIT**

#4 PROTECT THE CULTURE

CLAIM THAT IT'S IMPOSSIBLE TO BUILD A CULTURE WITHOUT MEETING IN PERSON

#5 HOPE FOR A RECESSION

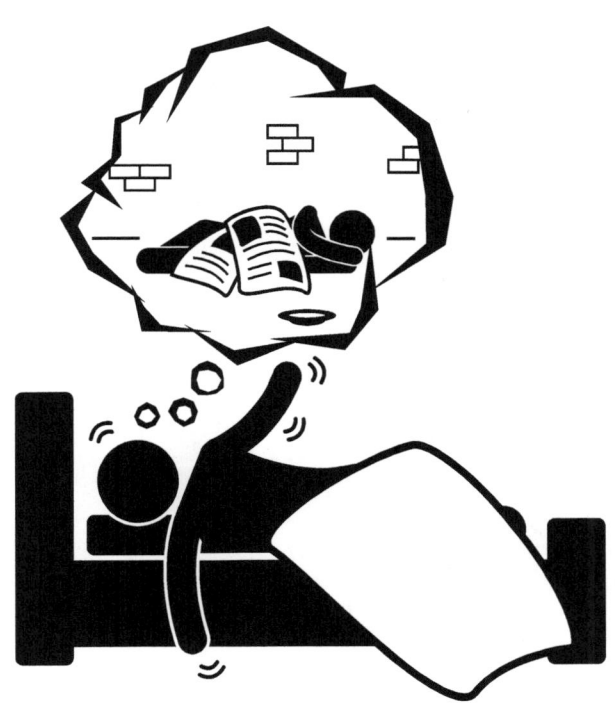

A RECESSION CAN SCARE EMPLOYEES BACK TO THE OFFICE

#6 THE A TEAM AND THE B TEAM

**MAKE IT CLEAR THAT THE PEOPLE WHO WORK IN THE OFFICE
BELONG TO THE A TEAM AND THE REST TO THE B TEAM**

#7 SIMULATE THE OFFICE

SCHEDULE REMOTE WORKERS INTO BACK-TO-BACK VIDEO MEETINGS SO THEY LONG BACK TO PHYSICAL MEETINGS

#8 CUT PAY FOR REMOTE WORKERS

**PAY EMPLOYEES BASED ON WHERE THEY LIVE
INSTEAD OF HOW THEY PERFORM**

#9 GIVE A FACE TIME BONUS

ENTICE EMPLOYEES BACK TO THE OFFICE WITH A CASH BONUS

#10 BUY A FOOTBALL GAME

A FOOTBALL GAME CAUSES EMPLOYEES TO RETURN TO THE OFFICE IN DROVES

"The real challenge in crafting strategy lies in detecting subtle discontinuities that may undermine a business in the future. And for that there is no technique, no program, just a sharp mind in touch with the situation."

– Henry Mintzberg

END NOTES

1. Bloom, N., Liang, J., Roberts, J., & Ying, Z. J. (2015). Does working from home work? Evidence from a Chinese experiment. The Quarterly Journal of Economics, 130(1), 165-218.

2. Cision PR Newswire. (2018, June 6). Workplace Distractions Cost U.S. Businesses $600 Billion Annually. Retrieved from https://www.prnewswire.com/news-releases/workplace-distractions-cost-us-businesses-600-billion-annually-300661864.html